COMMUNION SYMBOLS

YOUR CONNECTION TO NATURE'S SPIRIT

NITHYA CHELLAM

ISBN 979-888521810-8

We often forget that we are nature.
Nature is not something seperate from us.
So when we say whe have lost our connection to nature,
we have lost our connection to ourselves.

- Andy Goldsworthy

This book is dedicated to the elements of nature who so kindly talked to me through symbols
and allowed me to spread this work and "The Green Man" - the ever so God of the Forest who embodies the spirit of the trees and he who enables me to evolve with so much kindness.

.

Contents

Contents

Www.unearthoneearth.com

Foreword

True communion with Nature is possible when the energy sense is turned on and heightened.

You can feel the principles of nature even in a single leaf falling with its back to setting sun and you are moved by the songs of the birds in the morning. You come to realise that you were never alone, you have been surrounded by abundant energy of life.

You can achieve that kind of physical and spiritual renewal of energy that comes alone from the wonder of the nature by using these Communion symbols channelled by Nithya Chellam. Her strong belief in oneness and power of consciousness had gifted her with many talents and abilities.

This book is a exploration to commune with nature.

I am honoured to be a part of this book. May it be a gift to everyone to work towards oneness and consciousness.

Best wishes to the Author, the readers and the book.

Thank you

Shwetha Sathyanarayana

Preface

Earth and Nature gift us everything we have today and when work in communion with nature, you can recieve these gifts and know what a gift your life is.

Nature is ever so powerful and yet gifting, water can quench your thirst and nurture your body however the mighty ocean with water can drown you away. We live amongst such a powerful source that can kill you instantaneously if she so chooses, however she chooses to nurture us. Be amazed by the beauty of nature.

Each element of nature has gifted me symbols through which we can receive and perceive their energies in your hand. What if your touch has its own healing powers and if you combine the power of your touch with that of nature, you can use these to change your life and get more ease in your body.

These symbols were gifted to me with each element. I have explained what each element is and how to connect with them and also what benefits they can give you or anyone else's body. However the usages is not limited to only what i have given, you may be guided to use them differently or for other uses then what is mentioned in the book, you may use them according to your intuition.

Welcome to life changing tools in your hands, and do keep using them.

Be willing to perceive what they are and believe in your hands and yourself if you would like to see the best results, each of the symbol requires your touch for them to come alive and work for you, they will come willingly and will be honored by your touch.

The knowing that you are nature and nature gives you everyting and so what can you give in return to nature is what you are encouraged to function from. Nature, Earth, Universe and God, whatever you would like to call it never expects anything from you, however it would thrive on your laughther and your intent to ask for more possibilities. Would you be willing to be that from now onwards? To even consider the blessing that the air your breath is?

Acknowledgements

First and foremost, thank you to Nature itself.

Loads of gratitude to Parul Karki who did the illustrations for this book.

Gratitude to Joy Christy who helped with experimenting and writing the first communion symbols manual.

Gratitude to Sowmya Ajay and Shwetha Sathyanarayana for all thier encouragement in taking this work foreward.

Loads of gratitude for all the testimonials provided for this work done and all of my shamanic participants who have allowed me to be part of thier life and growth.

Prologue

Communion symbols are a set of symbols that you can use to heal yourself, heal others, raise your consciousness levels,also connect yourself to nature and heal nature.

Why should we be in communion with nature? Since we were born to be that way and receive from nature. Nature gifts us everything that we require, the earth provides us with all of our needs and we are dependent on the earth for our very living, the earth can continue to thrive without us. The earth is of abundant nature and continues to gift to us, despite how we treat her. If we treat her with gratitude then the nurturing that we can receive from her is much more.

Communion is a sense of peace of joy and the joy of peace and if you have this with your body and earth, your live will be so much more amazing.

Nowadays we have lost the art of being with nature and knowing that we are nature ourselves. These symbols will show up how nature is within you and how your body can very easily connect to nature and i would like for you to experience what i have had with these symbols in your own way. If you have learned Reiki it would be very easy for you to use these symbols, they also flow from your hands like reiki.

You do not need any special attunements to use these symbols since you are nature and also these are reqiured to reestablish the true connection you have with nature and also heal yourself and others. One may argue that if you are nature, why would we have to use the symbols? Well since this is one way for you to come to know who you are and how you can be all nature element from wherever you are even if the physical element is not available with you per se.

Welcome to a new and different adventure and as you already know - practice makes perfect so do practice as much as you can and it is ok if you cannot feel or perceive the symbols for the first few times or many times, just believe, have faith and allow them to show you how they work and how nature loves you if you allow it.

Each of the symbol given the next pages have been also provided with directions on how to draw them, you have to draw these symbols with one hand on the other hand without a pen or any instruments, the energy of the symbols will activate your palms and your hands. And then you use your hands to touch and heal or just for fun.

Also to be noted, the symbols have to only be drawn and you do not have to call out their names like we do in reiki symbols.

Also the symbols may not be perceived or work the same for everyone since everybody and every body are different, you are encouraged to find out a way that works for you.

Please follow the arrow mark for directions on how to draw the symbols for best results. Also use the symbols continuously for many days or months till you get the results, the time you have to use them for depends on your body and your receiving capacity.

Draw the symbols with your whole palm as opposed to just one finger so that they come alive with the overall energy of your hands. Allow them to energize you as you energize them.

ONE
SUN

Sun is a being that continuously evolves and contributes, the sunshine gives life to everything on the planet earth along with other elements. With the sun symbol you can call in the energy of the sun into your hand. This is the first communion symbol that was gifted to me from the universe. One of the most powerful symbols and easily perceived. The sun symbol will refresh and awaken you so it is best to use it in day time, if you use it at night then u may not be able to go to sleep. If you would like to stay awake and work at the night then you can use the sun symbol during night time too. Your body may feel hot but this is not fever.

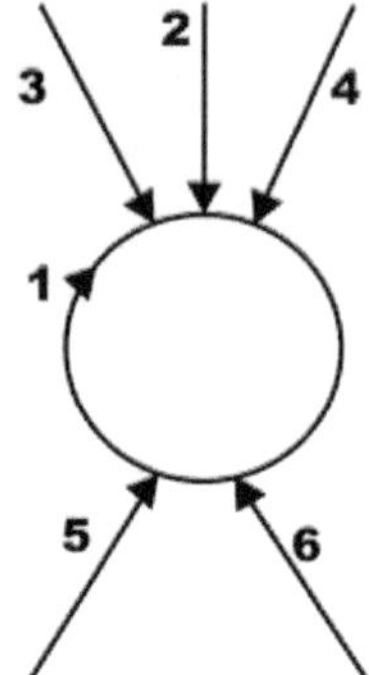

Sun Symbol

ꝒꝒꝒ

How to use sun:

1. Draw this on your hand and perceive the energy between your hands, you should usually feel the heat and the warmth of the sun
2. Keep your hands on your solar plexus chakra to increase your confidence
3. You can vizualize yourself and draw the symbol all around you with your thrid eye or imagination for your body to heat up and also let go of tiredness

ꝒꝒꝒ

Can also be used for:

1. Let go of tiredness
2. Tap into the energy of the sun
3. Helps become more energetic and refreshed to be awake, does not promote sleep
4. Helps with Vitamin D deficiency
5. Helps burn out negativity and also helps cleanse
6. Improves confidence when used on solar plexus chakra.
7. When feeling cold, helps keep warm
8. Keep away cold wind
9. Release pain in the body

TWO
MOON

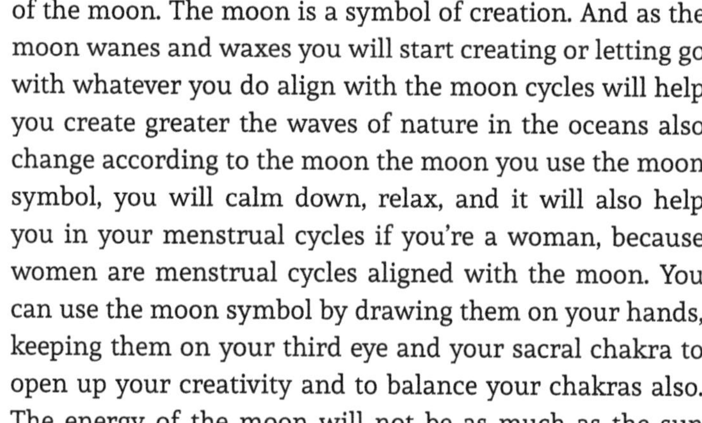

The Moon symbol will help you connect with the energies of the moon. The moon is a symbol of creation. And as the moon wanes and waxes you will start creating or letting go with whatever you do align with the moon cycles will help you create greater the waves of nature in the oceans also change according to the moon the moon you use the moon symbol, you will calm down, relax, and it will also help you in your menstrual cycles if you're a woman, because women are menstrual cycles aligned with the moon. You can use the moon symbol by drawing them on your hands, keeping them on your third eye and your sacral chakra to open up your creativity and to balance your chakras also. The energy of the moon will not be as much as the sun but yet it will be significant. If you can perceive it. You can use the moon symbol to feel calm, relaxed, start creating allowing new creations to grow to allow your new creations to grow. What you have to do is draw the moon symbol and visualize what you would like to actualize what you would like to manifest and do this for a few days till you feel that your subconscious has enough information to get this created. You can also use the moon symbol just to get the energies of the moon and feel the moon within you and how the moon would be if it were part of you. The moon does not have a light of its own, but it is so smart to be able to reflect what the sun has and change according to the need. So the moon will also help you tap into another infinite resource that can help you shape you up the way you like.

The whole moon is a symbol of abundance. It lets one tap into the power of creation. Makes you feel complete and fills you with happiness. Sign of new beginnings.

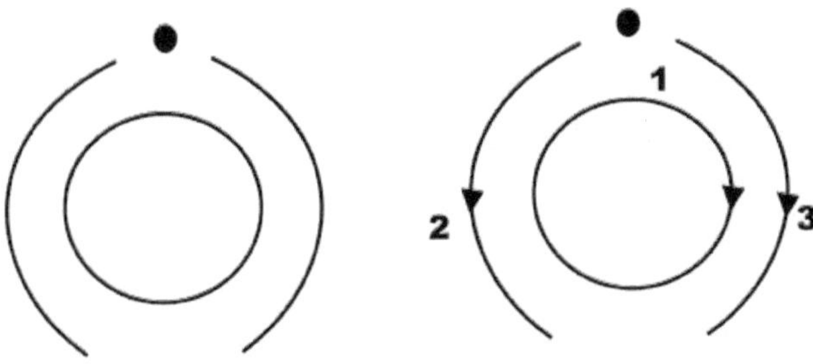

Moon Symbol

ↃↃↃ

<u>How to use Moon:</u>

1. Draw this on your hand and perceive the energy between your hands, you should usually feel cool or neutral.
2. Keep your hands on your Third Eye chakra during full moon and vizualize what you would like to let go.

3. Keep your hands on your Third Eye chakra during new moon and vizualize what you would like to create like imagine more money, abundance, getting good marks etc.
4. Keep your hands on your Sacral Chakra and ask for creation to flow through you and for your creative powers to be utilized well or just balance your Sacral Chakra.

Can also be used for:

1. Creating Abundance
2. Starting new Creation's
3. Feeling Complete
4. Happiness/Joy New beginnings
5. Balancing Third eye Chakra
6. Balancing Sacral Chakra
7. Clearing Confusion

THREE

EARTH

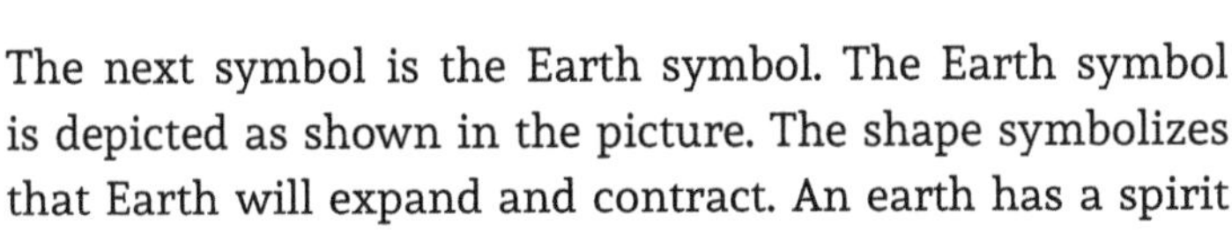

The next symbol is the Earth symbol. The Earth symbol is depicted as shown in the picture. The shape symbolizes that Earth will expand and contract. An earth has a spirit around it, which is the spirit of the earth. The earth gives us all the energies we require from the mud of Earth.

It is like having the sands and the mud in your hand and not the whole of the earth, but the land part.

So you can use the earth symbol to give yourself and your body a very good mud bath and it will revitalize your skin. The Earth symbol can also take away pain just like any other symbol, including the sun. You can also use it to tone up your body because when you put a mud pack on your body, your body will detoxify and start toning up. Earth can also help you with your teeth to make the roots of your teeth much stronger. The more you apply the earth symbol on your teeth, your gums will become stronger. It can also strengthen your bones as you touch the whole of your body with your hands. The Earth in combination with grass symbol can be used for hair growth also. The Earth symbol feels really wonderful and can be combined with any other symbol. If you combine the earth with rain, it will feel like the smell of rain and many people have noticed this and given the same feedback. Again you may or may not perceive it based on your level of consciousness and it is not wrong if you do not perceive it. With more practice it will show up the earth symbol can be used to rejuvenate any land if you would like to heal any dry land or any other sort of land that requires your attention. The Earth symbol will nurture whatever it touches. You can use it for healing plants also. And don't invite more stability and grounding in your life. drawing it on your feet and keeping it there for 510 minutes will enable that you are more connected to Earth and grounded. And this connection to earth is very very vital for our body because the body is after all, earth and all the other elements.

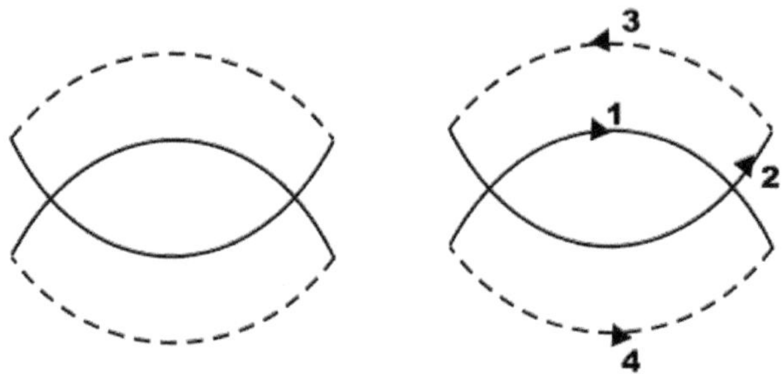

Earth Symbol

Earth symbol is an epitome of strength. It signifies nurturing, abundance, depth, freedom and love. Our mother earth lets everything flourish. It urges you to thrive, push yourself, and reach for your goals. Being humble and grounded is also a trait of the earth symbol. One could feel that the stored emotions are shed when using the earth symbol.

ÞÞÞ

<u>How to use:</u>

1. Draw the symbol on your hands and touch you feet for few minutes to get grounded or connected to earth.
2. Draw the symbol on your hands and keep your hands on your neck for 5 mins and then different positions of your face to get the effect of a mud facial on your skin.
3. You can use the symbol on your tummy to tighthen or tone up your tummy.

ÞÞÞ

<u>Can also be used for:</u>

1. Nurturing Your Body
2. Strengthening Bones
3. Deep Connection with Bones
4. Reach for your goals
5. Releae Stored emotions
6. Humble Flourishing

FOUR
HEART OF EARTH

The Heart of the Earth is the core energy of nurturing from the earth and can be used to perceive the expansive energy of earth and to know what is happening on mother earth. This symbol will feel different at different times based on what the earth is going through. When you use this symbol it is more about contributing to the earth rather than healing yourself. Our body and earth are very much connected, and the more earth thrives it enables us to thrive too.

The symbol with connect to the core of the earth and give your gratitude to her, when you use this symbol it works better if you express your gratitude to what mother earth has to offer to you in any way that you can.

You can use this in heart chakra to open and balance your heart.

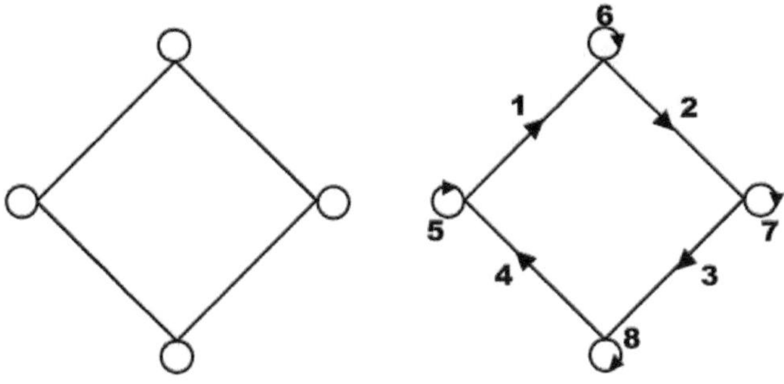

Heart Of Earth Symbol

Heart of the earth symbolizes Gratitude, for everything and every being in this earth. It imparts kindness, helps in controlling thoughts, enabling oneness with the earth and gives a sense of completion.

ᑭᑭᑭ

How to use the symbol:

1. Draw the symbol on your hands and keep it on your heart chakra for 10-15 mins whilst expressing gratitude to the earth
2. Draw the symbol and keep it in the place of your body that has any pain for few minutes.

ᑭᑭᑭ

Can also be used for:

1. Gratitude

2. Kindness
3. Controlling thoughts and emotions
4. Oneness with earth
5. Completion and wholeness
6. Release Pain the body

FIVE

STAR

The Star symbol will give you the energy in the power of the stars in the sky. All the stars put together will be available to you through the symbol. The star symbol will grant your wishes when you use this on your third eye and then visualize what you would like to create. visualize how you would like to see your wishes come true. It is said that a star can make your wishes wish come true. So use a star symbol to be able to actualize any wish that you have. You have to draw it I shown in the diagram with a circle and four triangles around the circle and this will give you the power and energy of the stars.

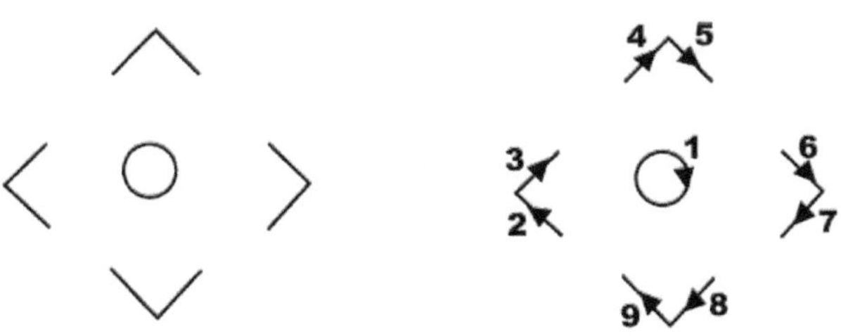

Star Symbol

Star also symbolizes light, shows the path and the way to go. Helps attain wish fulfillment and happiness. Stars indicate togetherness, as they keep planets and solar systems together.

ꝒꝒꝒ

<u>How to use:</u>

1. Draw the symbol on top of your crown chakra and allow the energy of the symbol to enter your third eye and then vizualize your wish, after vizualizing ask the star to grant your wish by chanting - "All the Stars, I request you to grant me my wish".

ꝒꝒꝒ

<u>Can also be used for:</u>

1. Shows the path
2. Light
3. Direction
4. Wish fulfillment
5. Smiles/happiness
6. Togetherness (keeps planets and solar system together)

SIX

WIND

The Wind symbol gives you the energy of the wind and the air. It enables your body to breathe better and also allows you to call upon the wind as a cool breeze to cool yourself down or as a hurricane to move things. It can also be used on your lungs to breathe better and to heal lungs. You can use this on your digestive system also to heal gastric problems. If your tummy is bloated you can also use the wind symbol to undo this. You can use the wind symbol to move plants or trees along with the movement of the wind.

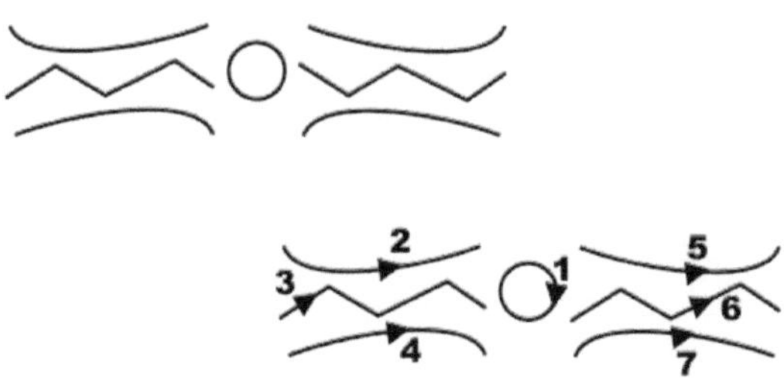

Wind Symbol

With the Wind symbol, we could sense the flow of the wind, a bit of warmth and the feel of flying high. The wind is related to throat chakra.

ϸϸϸ

How to use:

1. Draw the wind symbol on both your hands and keep one at the front and one at the back of the throat chakra and ask it to balance your throat chakra.
2. Draw the wind symbol on the chest area and ask it to heal your lungs by keeping your hands on your chest for 10 to 20 minutes.

ϸϸϸ

Can also be used for:

1. Flowing
2. Calling the Wind
3. Mild warmth
4. Throat chakra balancing
5. Flying high

SEVEN

EYE

The Eye symbol can be used to get clarity, to see clearly and also to heal your eyes. This symbol is mostly used on the eyes and the third eye and you can try this for any sort of eye disease. Please note that results from this symbol take more time as compared to other symbols. You can also use this to get the universe's perspective on life and living and increase your knowledge and awareness when you use this on your thymus.

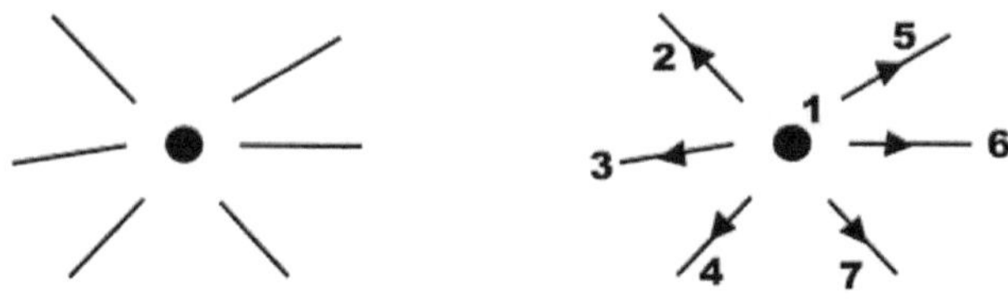

Eye Symbol

With the power of the Eye symbol, one can get a 360 degree vision, see through things and beings. It helps in revelation and leads to clarity. Leads to expansion of the being and vision.

ÞÞÞ

How to use:

1. Draw the eye symbol on both the hands and keep both hands on both eyes for 10 to 20 minutes to heal any eye problems.
2. Draw the eye symbol on both the hands and keep it on your third eye for clarity.

Draw the symbol on your palms and keep the palms on your thymus to increase your awareness.

ÞÞÞ

Can also be used for:

1. 360 degree vision
2. Eye opener
3. Clarity
4. Expansion of being and vision

EIGHT

RAIN

The Rain symbol was gifted to me by the rain when I was driving in my car and it was raining as I switched on the windshield wipers and his wiper went up and down I saw the symbol these beautiful amazing dots in the rain said this is how you can invoke and call me you can use the rain symbol to cool down places just as the earth cools down when the rain comes you can use the rain symbol to balance the water in your body you can use the rains in villages feel the energy of the beautiful rain upon your body the rain also brings in a lot of balancing and detoxification so this can be used to detoxify yourself and if you love singing and dancing in the rain I can also be used to bring your body alive the rain symbol is so amazing and when you draw these dots given in the sequence below please draw them with your whole palm rather than just a finger.

You can also use the rain symbol on the skies to request for it to start raining or to request to cool down the temperature of sun, when you use this on nature, it is request to nature to change but yet choose to do what is the best for nature itself and not a command over nature and most of the times nature will respond to your ask.

We have had cases where people where able to create rainfall by using the rain symbol.

Rain Symbol

Rain symbol signifies new beginnings, cleansing and feeling refreshed. As the raindrops touch the mother earth while falling from the sky, one is connected to the earth. Imparts pleasant fragrance and happiness.

<u>How to use:</u>

1. Draw the symbol on your top of your head with your third eye and allow it to shower rain and abundance over you.
2. Draw the symbol on your hands and place over any dry skin that you have or also on your tummy to reduce weight.

<u>Can also be used for:</u>

1. New beginnings
2. Cleansed Refreshed

3. Connecting to the earth
4. Fragrance
5. Happiness
6. Purification

NINE

WATER FALL

Waterfall is to get the energy of continuos flowing water that falls upon you to give you the joy of getting cleansed. You can this symbol to connect and fell the water fall energy on your body, to cleanse your skin and also ask the symbol to internally cleanse your blood.

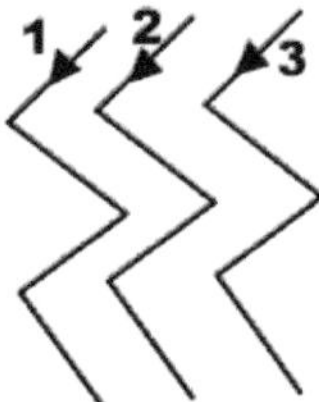

Water Fall Symbol

Waterfall helps in cleansing and imparts chillness. Signifies abundant blessings and the flow of richness.

<u>How to use:</u>

1. Draw the symbol on your top of your head with your third eye and allow it to shower waterfall and abundance over you.
2. Draw the symbol on your hands and place over any dry skin that you have or also on your tummy to reduce weight.

ᖰᖰᖰ

<u>Can also be used for:</u>

1. Cleansing the body, blood and mind
2. Cooling Down
3. Blessings from the universe
4. Flowing with Ease in life
5. Richness

TEN

WATER

Water is the most energy that can help cleanse and also liquify anything in the body, it can be used for any lumps in the body and also helps digest properly in case of any indigestion. It will feel like water flowing through your body when you use this and will help balance the water element in your body, it also helps balance the throat chakra and clears any communication blocks.

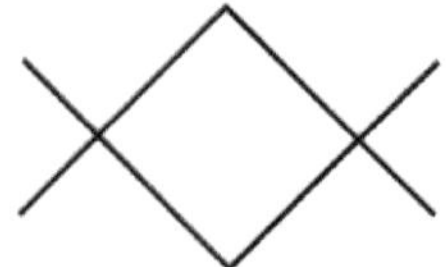

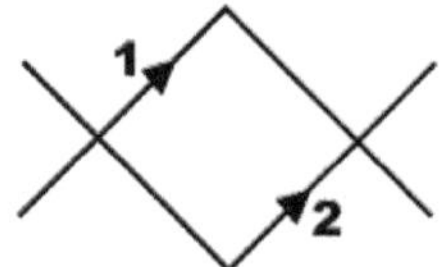

Water Symbol

ᑭᑭᑭ

How to use:

1. Draw the symbol on your top of your head with your third eye and allow it to shower waterfall and abundance over you.
2. Draw the symbol on your hands and place over any dry skin that you have or also on your tummy to reduce weight.
3. Draw the symbol on your hands and place on joints to make them more flexible, can help reduce artrithis.

Can also be used for:

1. Creation of life
2. Flowing with ease
3. Liquifying anything stiff or solid
4. Cherishing life
5. Balancing throat chakra
6. Enjoyment and pleasure
7. Heal any pain in the body

ELEVEN

RAINBOW

The Rainbow symbol will add a lot of color into your life and will give you what you require to make your life more lively. It has three semicircles and not seven because the colors are more prominent and this would be enough for you to call upon the symbol of the rainbow when you draw the symbol of the rainbow about your crown chakra and allow it to send you a lot of color throughout your whole body. You start feeling extremely good. And then you also attract more of abundance and money into your life. And you feel more lively with your body during the symbol is very, very beautiful.

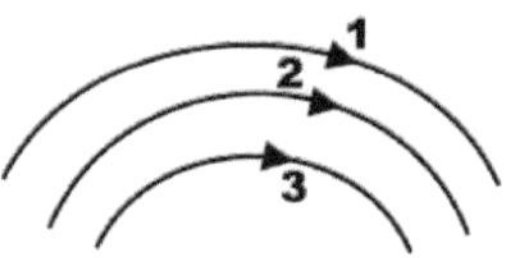

Rainbow Symbol

Symbol of colours, which indicates bonding of families Indicates oneness and raises the level of consciousness Helps Overcome depression also. The more usage of this symbol will help you move towards oneness with ease and joy.

ღღღ

How to use:

1. Draw the symbol on your top of your head with your third eye and allow it to shower color and abundance over you.
2. Draw the symbol on your thrid eye to add color and living to your life.
3. Draw the symbol and keep on your forehead to overcome stress and depression.

ღღღ

Can also be used for:

1. Colours
2. Bonding of families
3. Overcome depression
4. Oneness
5. Raised level of consciousness

TWELVE
CLOUD

The Cloud symbol will help you increase your creativity and imagination. You can use it on your third eye to get more clarity on your visions. It will create lightness in your body and your mind and enable you to get a feeling of flying.

Cloud Symbol

Symbol of adaptability, movement and absorption. Signifies imagination, creativity, and sense of floating high.

How to use:

1. Draw the cloud on your hands and keep it on your third eye and then visualize what you will like to create.
2. Draw the cloud on your hands and keep it on your third eye and ask the cloud to increase your imagination and creativity

ᑭᑭᑭ

Can also be used for:

1. Adaptability
2. Movement
3. Absorption
4. Floating high
5. Imagination
6. Creativity
7. Third eye balancing

THIRTEEN
TREE

The Tree symbol gives you the stability and grounding of a tree. This can be drawn along the spine from the bottom to the top. Starting with the symbols that represent the trunk, and then going into the leaf area. This will strengthen your spine, make it more straight and also help you resolve any back pain or spinal problems. When you use this continuously. This energy can also be drawn on the feet to give you the groundedness that you require. You can use the tree to start feeling more taller, really good about your body. Looking at yourself with confidence, changing the posture of your back or just get the loving energy that the tree has to offer you an energy that stands tall and continuously contributes to everyone.

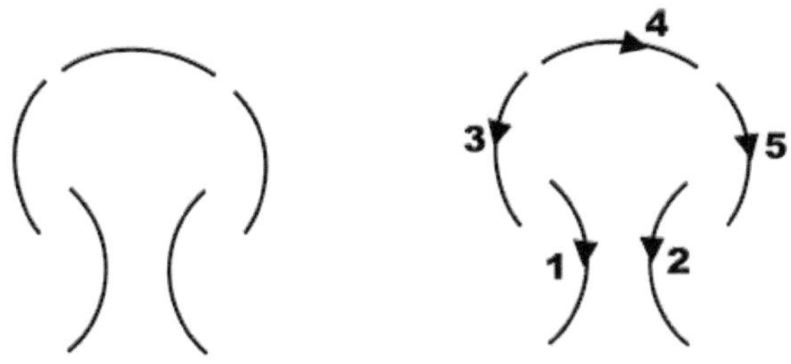

Tree Symbol

The tree symbol aids in grounding. Supports thriving. Symbol of prosperity and abundance.

ϷϷϷ

How to use:

1. Draw the tree symbol on your hands and then starting from the base of the spine. Keep it at the base of your spine for few minutes and keep going up till you cover the whole spine.
2. You can just visualize the whole picture of the tree drawn along the whole spine and just be with that energy.
3. You can also draw a tree on your feet and allow yourself to be grounded

ϷϷϷ

Can also be used for:

1. Grounding

2. Prosperity
3. Thriving
4. Reaching the top
5. Gifts/blessings

FOURTEEN

FIRE

The Fire symbol gives you the warmth and heat or fire in your hands. It also signifies a passion. If you draw it on your heart chakra or your solar plexus or both, it will help awaken that passion that you have hidden for so long and allow that to come alive. It can also be used just like the sun to heat the body. This is a milder version of the sun and does not give you as much as the sun does. But nevertheless can be used to balance the fire element in the body and also to heat up the body. The energy of fire will dance in your hands. You can use it on the spine to make the spine come alive. Also, you can use it on the skin to allow the skin to steam and get better.

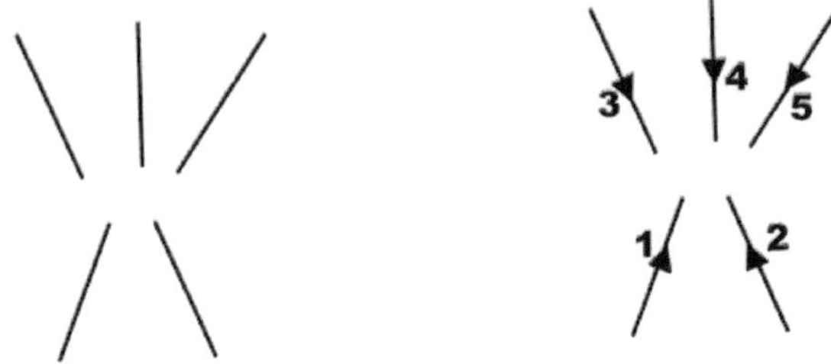

Fire Symbol

Tap into the power of fire and feel energized and renewed.

ꝒꝒꝒ

How to use:

1. Draw the symbol on both of your palms and keep it on your heart and solar plexus.
2. You can also use it alternatively on your root and your sacral together.
3. You can draw the fire symbol on your hands and keep each hand starting from the bottom of the spine. To the top of the spine to make the spine come alive.

ꝒꝒꝒ

Can also be used for:

1. Power (Solar Plexus)

2. Heat
3. Warmth
4. Passion

FIFTEEN

SKY

The Sky symbol will help you realize how far upward you and your being can expand and how vast you can truly be, this is just to experience what you can truly be if you are in communion with the sky. It can also help you get out of your ground reality and see how you can create when you focus on the larger picture.

Sky Symbol

Explore the vastness of the sky and go beyond the horizon.

How to use:

1. Draw the sky symbol on your palms and keep one palm on the crown chakra and one palm on the third eye chakra.

ღღღ

Can also be used for:

1. Vastness
2. Expansion

SIXTEEN

SPACE

The Space symbol will help you realize how far in all directions you and your being can expand and how vast you can truly be. How you are the space that can bring the change for you and others, it will help you get out of problems, emotions or thoughts and your mind level to be free to be able to clearly think about what you have to do next.

Space Symbol

Expand yourself and everything around you.

How to use:

1. Draw the sky symbol on your palms and keep one palm on the crown chakra and one palm on the third eye chakra.

ÞÞÞ

Can also be used for:

1. Expansive
2. Synchronized
3. Experiencing infiniteness
4. Releasing past issues
5. Churning out unwanted thoughts and memories

SEVENTEEN

GRASS

The Grass symbol when used on any part of the body will give a feeling of cushioning and support and the goodness of how you feel when you graze against the grass. You can use this on your feet also to connect with the grass on the earth.

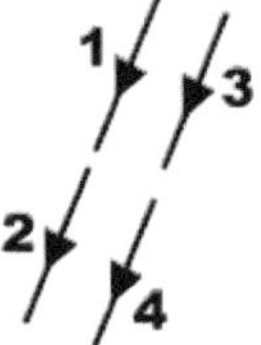

Grass Symbol

Feel the energy of grass and imbibe it.

<u>How to use:</u>

1. Draw the grass symbol on your palms and you can keep it on your wounds.
2. Draw the grass symbol on your palms and you can keep it on your scalp for hair growth.
3. Draw on both the feet to feel grounded.

<u>Can also be used for</u>

1. Bed/cushioning
2. Support
3. Smell
4. BeautyAbundance
5. Grounding
6. Hold the abundant rain
7. Smooth and even
8. Hair growth

EIGHTEEN

DEW

This symbol gives the freshness of the dew drops on the grass, you can use this to make your skin glow and get better, please don't use on wounds or dry skin, it is to make healthy skin healthier and also to enable yo to feel relaxed when you use it on your thrid eye or on the forehead.

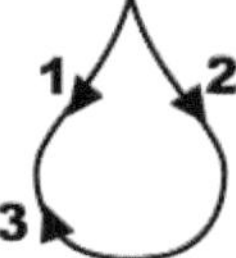

Dew Symbol

Imbibe the freshness of the dew within you.

ღღღ

<u>How to use:</u>

1. Draw the symbol on your hands and keep it on your forehead for few minutes to freshen you up and feel relaxed.
2. Draw the symbol on your hands and place it on the area of the skin that you would like to make smoother or healthier.

ᑭᑭᑭ

Can also be used for:

1. Freshness
2. Feeling rejuvenated
3. Feeling good

NINETEEN

SEED

The Seed symbol is to plant the seeds for a big creation in the future. It will the hold the DNA for what you have to create within it. You can think of what you would like to create and put it into the seed symbol and then visualize yourself planting the seed in the ground.

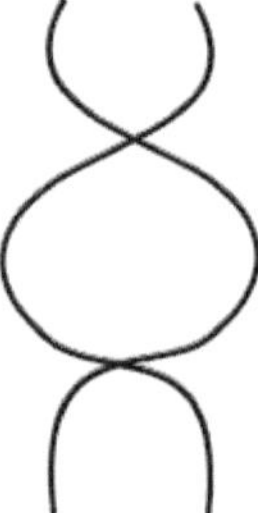

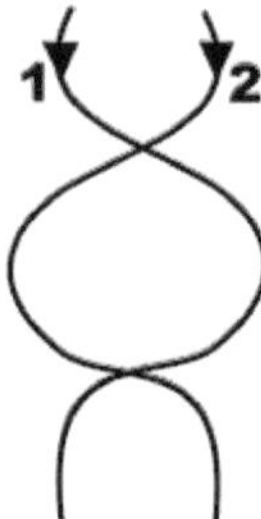

Seed Symbol

Plant seeds for magical creation.

How to use:

1. Visualize whatever you will like to create in between your hands. Draw the seed symbol on top of it and allow the vision to get into the strands of the seed symbol and alow the symbol to change into a seed. Now plant the seed in any ground that you like that is a metaphore for your subconscious mind.

ÞÞÞ

Can also be used for:

1. Healing genetic diseases
2. Creating new patterns
3. Duplicating existing patterns
4. Planting new ideas and visions

TWENTY

FLOW

The Flow symbol will open up all your chakras and balance them this symbol was gifted to me by the goddess TARA and also be called as TARA. Use this on each of your chakras to enable the proper flow of energies and open yourself up to fullfillment.

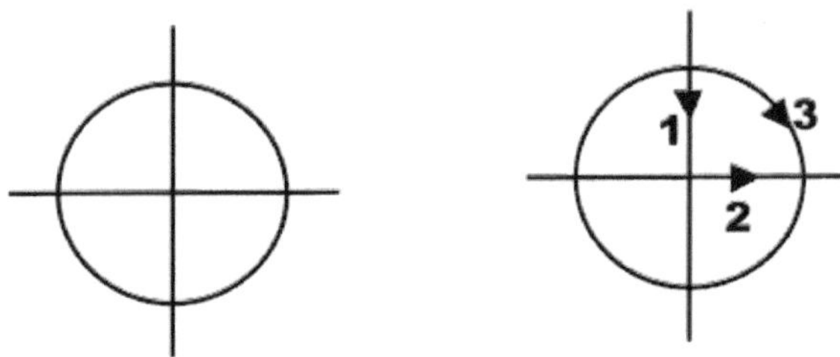

Flow Symbol

Open yourself up to bliss.

How to use:

1. Draw the symbol on your palm and keep it on each of your chakras for 10 minutes each.
2. Draw on your feet to open connection to earth.
3. Draw on your palms to open up receiving

Can also be used:

1. Opening palm chakras
2. Increasing receiving

TWENTY-ONE

MOUNTAIN

The Mountain Symbol will give you alot of strength it can be used when the body is shaky or shivering to stabalize the body. It can be used to strengthen the bones it can be used to heal pain also.

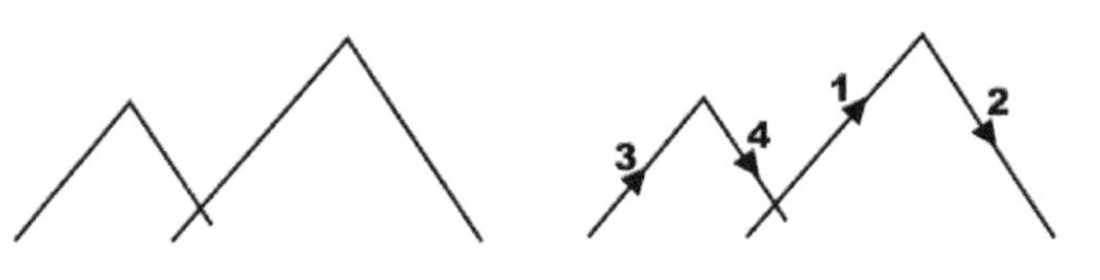

Mountain Symbol

ᘔᘔᘔ

How to use:

1. Draw the symbol on your hands and keep it in the weak part of your body.
2. Draw the symbol on your hands and keep it on the areas where you have pain in the body

<u>Can also be used for:</u>

1. Strengthening muscles
2. Strenghtening bones
3. Strenghtening the body

TWENTY-TWO

FERTILITY

The fertility symbol can be used to nurture the planted seeds like in the next steps of your vision, like charging your business to grow or on pregnant women for the baby to keep thriving and growing better.
This symbol has to be used on something that has already started to make it more fertile.

Fertillity Symbol

Let the sown seeds lead to fruition.

How to use:

1. Draw the symbol on your palms and keep it on your sacral chakra.
2. Draw the symbol and keep it on your uterus area to heal any menstrual pain.

ᑭᑭᑭ

Can be used for:

1. Blooming
2. Flourishing
3. Conception

TWENTY-THREE

FLOWER

Flower symbol gives to the creativity to create with color and fragrance, it also allows you body to become more feminine with nurturing energy of flowers, you can use this around your sacral chakra and uterus area to shape your body and make your skin more smooth.

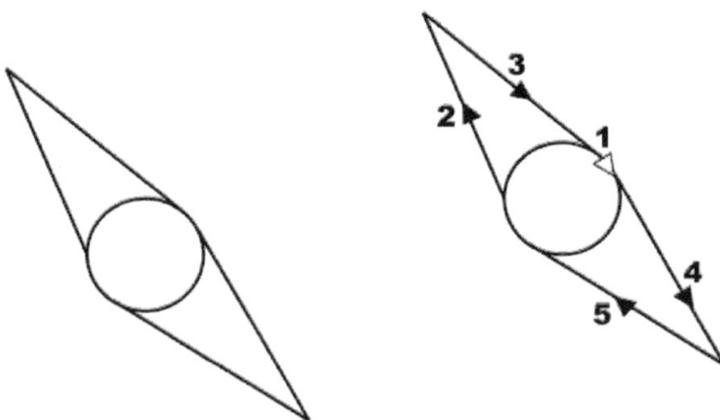

Flower Symbol

Imbibe the fragrance and beauty of flower within you.

How to use:

1. Draw the symbol on your hands and place on uterus area and sacral chakras.
2. Draw the symbol on your hands and place them all over your face.
3. Draw the symbol on your hands and keep on your navel for 10-15 minutes.

Can also be used for:

1. Joy
2. Beauty facial for face
3. Pleasant smell
4. Add color to your projects

TWENTY-FOUR

PRESENCE

Presence is the symbol that allows you to come back to the now and to be in the present. The magic of the present and your presence is what you should be looking for. This symbol can be used on your forehead or mind area to let go of the past and future and ground yourself to the magic of the presence. The infinite gratitude that you can be for all you have and the infinite awareness you can be when you are out of all judgement. The gift of the now is what this symbol can offer you and also show you how you can be more of yourself as an expansive energy.

Presence Symbol

ღღღ

How to use:

1. Draw the symbol on your hands and place on your forehead to feel expanded and come back to the now.
2. Draw the symbol on your heart to feel the gratitude you have for now.

ღღღ

Can also be used for:

1. Being in the now
2. More Presence
3. Intensity of your being

TWENTY-FIVE

ANIMAL

This symbol can be used to invoke the energy of any animal in your hands including fishes, amphibians, reptiles, birds and insects too. You have to draw the symbol between both of your palms and then visualize the animal you would like to call upon for eg: you can call Lion for emotional strength, you can call eagle to give you a higher vision and then just allow the energy of the animal to get imbibed into every cell of your body and enjoy the experience, the spirit animals may also give you messages or symbols when you use this.

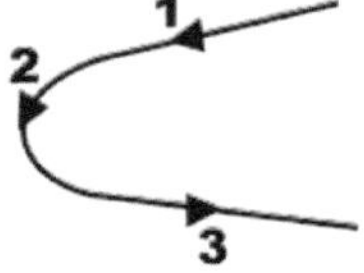

Animal Symbol

How to use:

1. Draw the symbol in both palms, keep your hands close together and invoke with the name, the animal you would like to connect too and just be with the animal, feel it's energy in your body and look out for any visions or messages.
2. Draw the symbol in both palms, keep your hands close together and invoke with the name, the animal you would like to connect too and just be with the animal and you can ask the animal to help you with any area in your life.

Can also be used for:

1. Connecting with all animal energies
2. Getting strengh of the animal

TWENTY-SIX

MALE LEAF

The male leaf is to be drawn all over the spine starting from the base of the spine to the top and we keep continuing the two strokes more than 6 till you reach the top of the spine near the base of the neck.

This just helps strengthen the spine and makes the spine feel good. Please make sure to use the female leaf symbol after you finish the male leaf symbol on the spine, you can do 1 - 5 rounds of both the symbols.

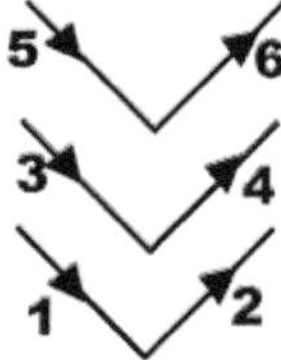

Male Leaf Symbol

TWENTY-SEVEN

FEMALE LEAF

The female leaf is to be drawn all over the spine starting from the top of the spine to the bottom and we keep continuing the two strokes till you reach the base of the spine near the tail bone.This just helps strengthen the spine and makes the spine feel good. Please make sure to use the male leaf symbol before you start the female leaf symbol on the spine, you can do 1 - 5 rounds of both the symbols.

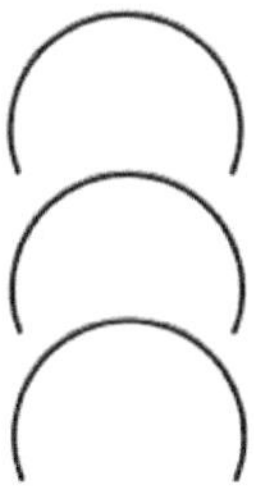

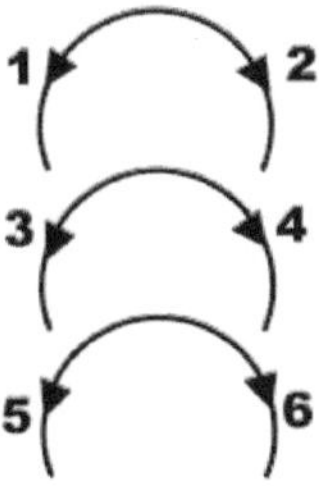

Female Leaf Symbol

TWENTY-EIGHT

COMBINING SYMBOLS

You can combine any or all of the symbols together since all of nature exists together and to do that you have to draw the symbols on top of each other on your hands and use them.

For eg: If you draw the earth and then rain on it or vice versa, you can feel the smell of earth before it rains.

You can combine water, waterfall and rain and use it on your body to reduce the extra weight in any area of the body.

Earth and water combined will be like applying healing mud all over your body.

Sun and water will give the effect of the sun but a little more cooler than the normal sun.

Earth and Grass combined can be used on the scalp for hair growth.

Grass and Dew symbols can be combined and used together to give freshness and relaxation and also to enable you to sleep well.

Testimonials

ᑭᑭᑭ

I had amazing experience using the communion symbols. My plants grew much faster after using theses symbols. I am using them to heal my relationships. I could connect to the animals without taking shamanic journey using these symbols. Thank you Nithya for these amazing symbols.

- Shwetha Sathyanarayana

ᑭᑭᑭ

I experienced the magic of communion symbols when it was used for healing the lake near our house .In 2018 the lake had totally dried up and fishes were dying .After few sessions of healing ,there was some rains after the long dry spell .Also The community near the lake started taking initiatives to revive the lake. Eventually the lake is now fully back to its original condition.

Many times I have used communion symbols to call for rains, sometimes I have used communion symbols to warm up the room or to call out the sun, when there are heavy rains which can lead to flooding or endanger people. However I have noticed the communion symbols are most powerful when used in communion with nature ,rather than out of personal will.

They are pure magic !!!! I am grateful to Nithya for teaching them .

- Shilpa somasundaram

ᑭᑭᑭ

My mother Pushpa Raheja aged 79 years suffered from diarrhea for over a year and half. We tried all medicines, nothing worked. She would be ok one day and worse on other days. The doctors prescribed many antibiotics but nothing would restore her health. She had lost all hope of getting well. I used the water symbol and earth symbol (as guided by Nithya) and she bounced back to being normal in a week or two. I don't have words to express gratitude to Nithya for this guidance. Using the communion symbols has saved my mother's life. She is happy and cheerful now.

With deep gratitude,

- Vandana Rajpal

♡♡♡

I have used water symbol on my solar plexus chakra. This has helped me releasing stored emotions and feel better within a few minutes of using this symbol. Another one i use is the sun symbol, which gives me confidence and clarity.

- Sowmya Ajay

Unearth One Earth

Unearth One Earth is my organization that is a "Spirit School of Evolution".
The focus is on working with nature spirits to make oneness a reality on this planet and for everyone to know the truth of who they are. Shamanic Healing and Communion Symbols are some of the streams available for you here.

The fox spirit animal helps you to find what you would like and also dig hence representing unearthing and we will engage the fox and spirit of earth to live as One Earth.

Spirit School Of Evolution - Be One With Earth

Next Steps

If you would like to explore more on these symbols, how to use them exhaustively, how to do body massages with them, more on shamanic healing or just learn to become more of yourself, do touchbase with me through my website www.nithyachellam.com or www.unearthoneearth.com. There are special courses and classes available to explore more of these.

Hope to see you soon, magical being!!

Gratitude

My Sincere gratitude to you for choosing to have a copy of this book and i hope that it brings you as much fun and joy that it did for me or more.

- Nithya Chellam

www.ingramcontent.com/pod-product-compliance
Ingram Content Group UK Ltd.
Pitfield, Milton Keynes, MK11 3LW, UK
UKHW040011200726
13854UKWH00001B/154

9 798885 218108